The Art of Dressing Long Hair

Guy Kremer and Jacki Wadeson

PHOTOGRAPHY: BARRY COOK

City&
Guilds

DENMAN

THOMSON

GK
Guy Kremer

HABIA
Hairdressing And Beauty Industry Authority

THOMSON

British Library Cataloguing-in-Publication Data
A catalogue record for this book is available from the British Library

ISBN 1-86152-939-2

First edition published by Thomson Learning 2004

Designed and typeset by LewisHallam

Printed in Italy by G. Canale & C.

Contents

Acknowledgements

Hair: Guy Kremer of Guy Kremer International, Winchester www.guykremer.com
Assisted by: Charlie Manns, Guillaume Vappereau, Stacey Egan
Brushes and combs: Denman International Ltd www.denmanbrush.com
Electrical equipment: BaByliss Professional
Styling products: L'Oreal Professionnel
Hair pieces: Trendco, www.wigsattrendco.co.uk
Clothes: Moda Rosa, Alresford, Hants
Hair accessories: Irresistible Headdresses, www.irresistibleheaddresses.com
Photography: Barry Cook
Editor: Jacki Wadeson

With special thanks to:

Jonathan S King of Denman International; Ginny Hicks of BaByliss;
Rosie Wild, Julia Pettit and Patricia Elliot of Moda Rosa, Alresford, Hants

Introduction

The internationally renowned Guy Kremer is a charismatic blend of Gallic charm and innovative talent. Famous for his elegance and style, his hairdressing expertise is seen regularly in the *Daily Express, You & Your Wedding, Bride and Groom, Hello, OK, Cosmopolitan* and *Good Housekeeping*.

An incredible showman, he stuns audiences with gravity defying chignons perfectly entwined to complement couture dresses from the crème de la crème of the fashion world. His work for celebrity designers Isabel Kristensen and Maria Grachvogel brings his Parisian style to audiences of catwalk and charity shows around the world.

Voted one of the Top 75 Educators of the Century by USA industry bible, *Modern Salon*, he is in great demand for long hair seminars all over the world. He loves sharing his skills, and has the uncanny knack of being able to combine the classic with the funky, to create styles that transform the very fabric of hair. The key to Guy's long hair work is its simplicity. Here he shows, in simple step by steps, just how easy it is to master the world of long hair and create fashionable, classic, romantic and classy looks for your clients.

Jacki Wadeson

ANOUSKA

1. Before.

2. Trim fringe to give a neat line.

3. Scoop hair into a ponytail on crown. Secure with a covered band.

4. Smooth ponytail using a hot curl brush and heat from hairdryer.

5. Divide ponytail into three equal strands and plait to ends.

6. Coil plait round ponytail and secure in place with grips.

7. Match hairpiece to hair colour.

8. Grip hairpiece in place to base of ponytail.

9. Divide hairpiece into three equal strands and begin to plait.

10. Continue plaiting down to ends of hairpiece.

11. Coil plait round and secure in place with pins.

12. Repeat process using another hairpiece, but this time allow a section to loop down over one ear. Mist with hairspray.

OPPOSITE Coat: Matthew Williamson at Moda Rosa, Alresford, Hants

CANDY

1. Before.

2. Use a grooming brush to smooth hair into a ponytail at one side.

3. Secure ponytail in covered hooked band making sure you keep the tension whilst holding the hair.

4. Take a small section of hair and use to cover the band, secure in place with grips.

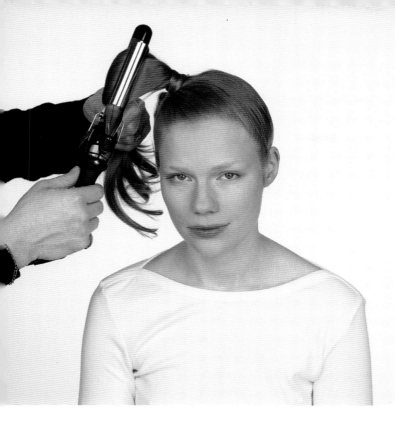

5. Smooth hair using a curling iron, 24mm diameter. Work from roots down to ends.

6. Sleekness rather than curl is achieved with this type of tong. This forms basis for the style.

7. Take a fine section of hair from ponytail and backcomb starting 5cm from ends, work to roots.

8. Backcomb remaining ponytail hair and mist with fixing spray.

9. Divide hair into two and form one half into round shape, smooth just a little and secure in place.

10. Take 2nd section and insert pin into base twisting as you insert to ensure it is secure.

11. Push pin right in – see position – this is most important as it helps to hold style in place. Smooth over hair to form shape.

12. Mist with fixing spray whilst shaping the hair with a tail comb to give candyfloss texture. Hold in a fine hair net.

OPPOSITE Top and skirt: Matthew Williamson at Moda Rosa, Alresford, Hants
Hair accessory: Irresistible Headdresses

EMMANUELLE

1. Before.

2. Use a paddle brush to dry hair, brushing continuously as you dry for a smooth finish.

3. Straighten hair, a section at a time, using straightening irons.

4. Smooth serum through outer layers of hair to banish any flyaway ends.

5. Brush hair forwards from crown.

6. Smooth hair into a slightly offset ponytail at hairline.

7. Clasp hair in hand, twist clockwise and secure base of the twist.

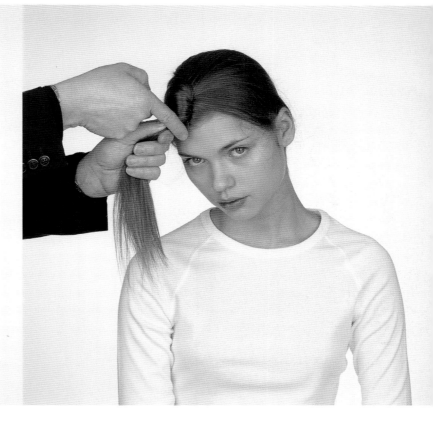

8. Secure with grip at base of the twist.

9. Secured hair.

10. Backcomb ponytail from midlengths towards roots.

11. Fold over holding ends with hand.

12. Tuck in ends and secure with grips.

OPPOSITE Dress: Paddy Campbell at Moda Rosa, Alresford, Hants

MELODY

1. Before.

2. Smooth hair straight using a paddle brush and heat from hairdryer.

3. Dispense a few drops of serum to palm of one hand and work through hair.

4. Use a grooming brush to smooth hair to side of head. It is essential to use a bristle/nylon mix brush to eliminate static.

5. Hold ponytail tight and secure in a covered band.

6. Smooth ponytail hair.

7. Take a small section from ponytail, wrap round base of ponytail and secure in place.

8. Loop ponytail and secure loop to head as shown.

9. Loop in position with ends of ponytail hanging down.

10. Take ends round back and secure where shown with end of styling comb.

11. Comb ends forward to form a 'fake' fringe.

12. Push hair accessory into place.

OPPOSITE Blouse and skirt: Clements Ribeiro at Moda Rosa, Alresford, Hants
Headdress: Irresistible Headdresses

VERITY

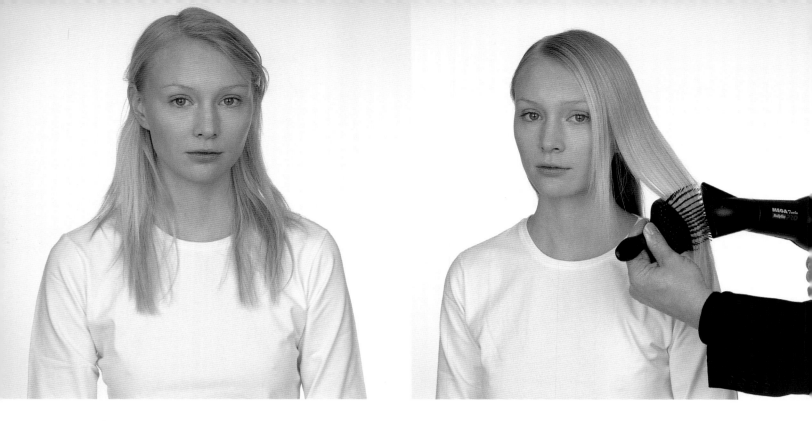

1. Before.

2. Smooth hair using a paddle brush and heat from hairdryer.

3. Maximise smoothness using straightening irons from roots to ends.

4. Smooth hair into a ponytail at nape of neck and secure with a covered band.

5. Take a small section of hair and use to wrap round base of ponytail.

6. Mist with hairspray.

7. Backcomb ponytail finishing 2.5cm from ends.

8. Shows ponytail backcombed.

9. Insert pin into ponytail and twist round, then pin so that it
   is lifted up a little.

10. Mist with hairspray.

11. Take a small hairpiece that matches hair and backcomb in
    same way.

12. Pin hairpiece in place on crown and dress onto crown. Pin
    in place.

OPPOSITE Suit: Paule Ka at Moda Rosa, Alresford, Hants

ATTICA

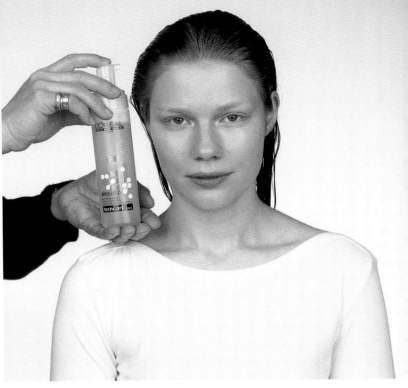

1. Before.

2. Apply mousse to towel dried hair.

3. Rough dry hair using a paddle brush and nozzle attachment on dryer, which concentrates heat flow.

4. Finish drying hair using a hot curl brush to smooth hair and eliminate static.

5. Centre part hair, then divide off crown hair and secure into a high ponytail using a covered band.

6. Insert bun ring by putting hand through centre and clasping ponytail then pulling hair through.

7. Secure bun ring in place using grips. Push grips in horizontally to give maximum security.

8. Build 'scaffolding' round bun ring by inserting pins in upright positions as shown.

9. Divide ponytail into two and wrap first section round bun ring. Note how the 'scaffolding' helps keep hair in place. Secure with pins at base of bun ring.

10. Remove pin scalfolding, leaving one pin in place as shown.

11. Take a small section from remaining ponytail hair, coil round fingers as shown and form into a curl. Secure with a grip. Curl remaining hair in same way.

12. Smooth the front section hair behind ears using using a tail comb leave the tendrils to fall freely.

OPPOSITE Dress: Patric Casey at Moda Rosa, Alresford, Hants
Headdress: Irresistible Headdresses

BETHANY

1. Before.

2. From a centre parting brush hair behind ear and secure in a covered band.

3. Push bun ring over ponytail so that is it close to head and secure with grips.

4. Divide ponytail into five sections and set on heated rollers. Leave until completely cool before removing.

5. Remove rollers and allow hair to fall into open curls.

6. Twist hair into a coil, secure into centre of bun ring. This hair will be released in Step 11.

7. Select a hairpiece that matches natural colour and use grips to secure base of hairpiece to bun ring.

8. Divide hairpiece into three equal strands.

9. Plait hair right down to ends.

10. Twist plait round bun ring.

11. Remove ponytail hair from bun ring, divide into two. Loop one section upwards into a curl and pin.

12. Twist and coil remaining section into a curl and pin in place.

OPPOSITE Dress: Jenny Packham at Moda Rosa, Alresford, Hants
Hair accessory: Irresistible Headdresses

BONNIE

1. Before.

2. Dispense mousse onto a vent brush then evenly distribute through hair from roots to ends.

3. Allow length of hair to sit in diffuser cup of dryer, the heat will gently penetrate the hair and curls will begin to form.

4. Continue drying in same manner, working round head, until you have achieved lots of volume and texture.

5. Create a zigzag parting from front hairline to crown as shown.

6. Secure hair at one side in covered band.

7. Continue zigzag parting down back of head to nape, then secure hair at other side in a covered band.

8. Note that the two ponytails are asymmetric.

9. Take a strand of hair from one ponytail and wrap around band to cover. Repeat for other ponytail.

10. Backcomb ponytail using fingers, then twist into a cone shape and secure. Backcomb other ponytail in same way.

11. Twist backcombed hair into a cone shape and secure with grips as before.

12. Shape cone using a tail comb to lift and finish. Mist with hairspray to hold shape.

OPPOSITE Dress: Jenny Packham at Moda Rosa, Alresford, Hants
Hair accessory: Irresistible Headdresses

CHLOE

1. Before.

2. Part hair at side then smooth crown hair into a high ponytail. Divide ponytail into five and set on heated rollers.

3. Set side hair on heated rollers as shown, i.e. two rollers on smaller side section, three rollers on large side section.

4. Completed heated roller pli. Mist with hairspray and leave rollers to cool completely.

5. Carefully remove rollers from sides and allow curls to fall freely. Now remove rollers from crown in same way.

6. Smooth hair using a grooming brush which will help to eliminate any static and tendency to flyaway.

7. Clip side hair out of the way and take a square section on crown. Twist hair in a clockwise direction for 5cm.

8. Use tail comb to hold twist at root area, bend twist forwards and secure with crossed grips.

9. Loop ends of hair into a curl and secure with a grip, form ends round base of curl and secure.

10. Curl remaining crown hair in same way. Smooth one side of nape hair upwards and grip, form ends into a curl.

11. Smooth other side of nape hair upwards and grip, form ends into a curl as before and grip.

12. Smooth one side of front hair to centre back and grip, form ends into curls and grip. Repeat for other side.

OPPOSITE Dress: Amanda Wakeley at Moda Rosa, Alresford, Hants
Hair accessory: Irresistible Headdresses

EVITA

1. Before.

2. Part hair in centre, brush straight back to nape of neck and secure in a covered band.

3. Smooth ponytail using a hot curl brush and heat from dryer.

4. Divide ponytail into three equal sections.

5. Plait down to ends of hair.

6. Twist plait round base of ponytail and secure with grips.

7. Take a matching hairpiece and plait down length.

8. Secure base of plaited piece to base of ponytail and grip in place.

9. Twist plaited piece round plaited bun.

10. Secure end of plaited piece with a grip.

11. Take another matching hairpiece, secure to base of original
ponytail and coil and pin as first piece.

12. Secure with pins and mist with hairspray.

OPPOSITE *Dress: Jenny Packham at Moda Rosa, Alresford, Hants*
Hair accessory: Irresistible Headdresses

AUDREY

1. Before.

2. Blow-dry hair using concentrator nozzle on hairdryer and a hot curl brush.

3. Set hair on heated rollers.

4. Completed heated roller pli.

5. Smooth fringe using a paddle brush.

6. When hair is completely cool remove heated rollers.

7. Use a grooming brush to smooth hair as this helps to eliminate static.

8. Backcomb first top section of hair.

9. Backcomb sides of hair.

10. Completed backcombing.

11. Use a grooming brush to smooth hair from right hand side to centre back, tuck in ends and secure with grips to create a French pleat.

12. Smooth right then left hand side of hair to centre back and secure with grips.

OPPOSITE Dress: Paule Ka at Moda Rosa, Alresford, Hants
Hair accessory: Irresistible Headdresses

CLARIS

1. Before.

2. Smooth hair into a ponytail at nape of neck and secure with a hooked band.

3. Tong ponytail hair starting at the roots.

4. Work tong down length taking care not to buckle ends.

5. Ponytail tonged.

6. Take a fine section of hair and wrap round base of ponytail, secure with grips.

7. Divide ponytail into two sections, clip top section up.

8. Divide lower section into two.

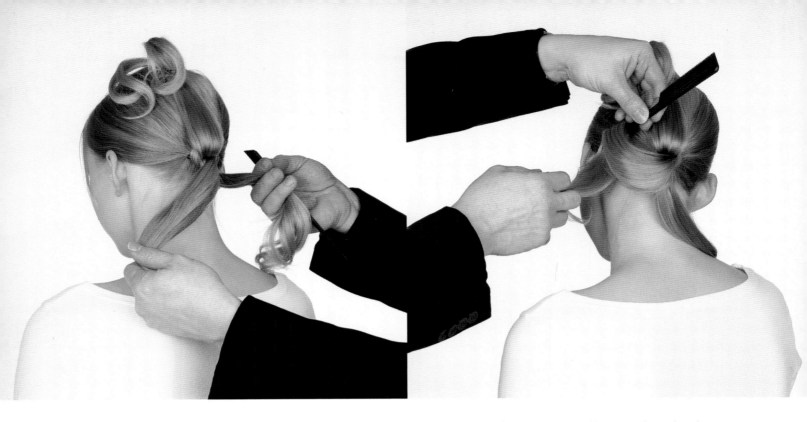

9. Cross over sections.

10. Backcomb left hand section and loop to side, tuck ends in and pin.

11. Work other lower section in same way.

12. Divide top reserved section into three and work in same way.

OPPOSITE Suit: Georges Rech at Moda Rosa, Alresford, Hants
Hair accessory: Irresistible Headdresses

GRACE

1. Before.

2. Use a straightening brush and heat from the dryer to straighten hair.

3. Take fine section of hair at one side.

4. Use section and wrap around to secure hair in ponytail at base of neck.

5. Secure ponytail with grips.

6. Divide ponytail into two equal sections.

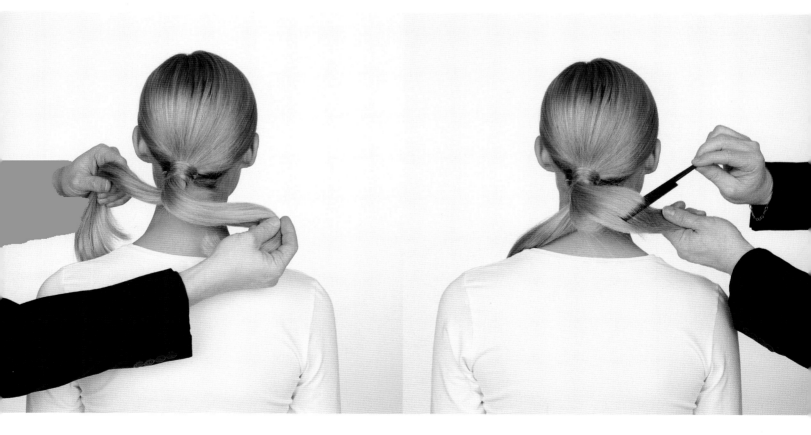

7. Cross over sections.

8. Backcomb one section at base.

9. Smooth backcombed section into a large curl and mist with hairspray.

10. Secure with grips.

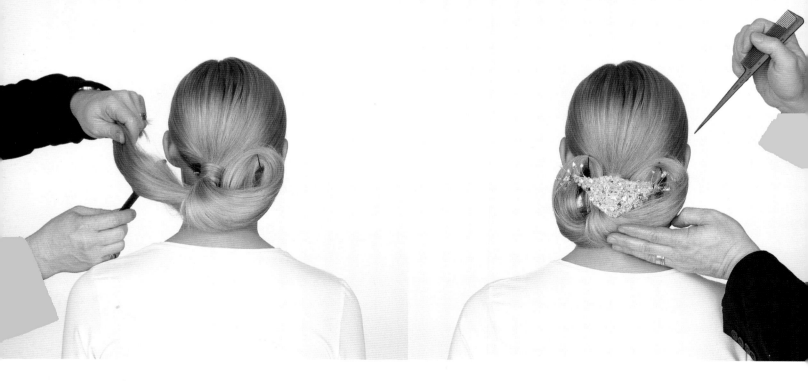

11. Repeat for other side.

12. Push hair accessory into place.

OPPOSITE Suit: Renato Nucci at Moda Rosa, Alresford, Hants
Hair accessory: Irresistible Headdresses

TIFFANY

1. Before.

2. Apply mousse distributing from roots to ends of hair.

3. Trim fringe for a really polished finish.

4. Dry hair using diffuser attachment on dryer and a hot curl brush.

5. Secure hair in a high ponytail, secure with a covered band.

6. Ponytail secured.

7. Place bun ring at base of ponytail.

8. Secure bun ring using grips.

9. Continue working round in same manner.

10. Match a hairpiece to natural shade.

11. Secure hairpiece into bun ring winding round the bun ring to create a pillar-box. Secure ends with grips.

12. Smooth ponytail, blend into hairpiece and grip in place.

ZOE

1. Before.

2. Apply serum through hair from roots to ends to control curl.

3. Take a fine section of hair and smooth between fingers.

4. Twist hair round fingers.

5. Pin into a flat curl.

6. Do another flat curl in same way.

7. Repeat all over head.

8. Dry using diffuser until hair is completely dry. Switch to cold shot at end to set the hair before releasing pins.

9. Section off top hair and hold in hand.

10. Secure at crown at centre back with crossed pins.

11. Take lower hair from right hand side, smooth over and insert a row of pins up centre back.

12. Wrap hair from left hand side round, tuck in ends and pin. Smooth remaining hair into top of 'formed cone' and pin.

OPPOSITE Suit: Renato Nucci at Moda Rosa, Alresford, Hants
Hair accessory: Irresistible Headdresses

ANASTASIA

1. Before.

2. Mousse is applied to damp hair and distributed from roots to ends.

3. Hair is blow-dried a section at a time using a paddle brush.

4. A grooming brush is used to smooth hair into a high ponytail.

5. Secure hair in ponytail using a covered band.

6. Set ponytail on heated rollers and leave until completely cool.

7. Release heated rollers and take a small section of hair and wrap round base of ponytail.

8. Secure with a grip.

9. Take a piece of hair padding.

10. Use as a roller on ponytail hair.

11. Curve round to form a high bun.

12. Secure with grips.

OPPOSITE Dress and wrap: Renato Nucci at Moda Rosa, Alresford, Hants
Hair accessory: Irresistible Headdresses

ASTRA

1. Before.

2. Apply mousse to roots to give volume and lift.

3. Dry hair using volumising brush, smoothing hair from roots to ends as you blow-dry. Use concentrator nozzle on dryer to speed up the drying process.

4. Create a front parting, take a rectangular section on the bias from hairline to crown as shown.

5. Twist this entire section of hair clockwise from roots to ends. Mist with hairspray to eliminate stray ends.

6. Continue to twist the hair which will double back on itself to form a coil.

7. Secure the coil to the scalp using a grip. This is the first coil completed.

8. Continue working in same way until all front section hair is twisted, coiled and gripped into place.

9. Continue working with crown hair but taking larger sections to work with.

10. Final coil on crown section being completed.

11. Proceed into nape area taking a diagonal section, overdirecting towards the crown, twist and coil then secure into place. Repeat for other side.

12. Finally fix any stray ends using pins to complete the finished look.

OPPOSITE Dress: Jenny Packham at Moda Rosa, Alresford, Hants
Hair accessory: Irresistible Headdresses

CELINE

1. Before.

2. Smooth hair using concentrator attachment on dryer and a hot curl brush.

3. Leave fringe out and scoop hair into a high ponytail. Secure with covered band.

4. Set ponytail on heated rollers, mist with hairspray. Leave to cool.

5. Remove rollers and allow curls to form.

6. Take a small section of hair and wrap round base of ponytail. Grip in place.

7. Take one curl and backcomb at roots.

8. Form into a curl and pin in place, leaving ends of curl loose.

9. Make two more curls at front in same way. Take back section of hair and curl forward.

10. Secure in place to curl already made, i.e. making a second layer of curls.

11. Make another curl in same way.

12. Comb fringe forward but to the side.

OPPOSITE Dress: Jenny Packham at Moda Rosa, Alresford, Hants
Hair accessory: Jenny Packham

ISABELLA

1. Before.

2. Work serum all through hair to smooth cuticle.

3. Begin drying by allowing hair to sit in diffuser cup of dryer.

4. When hair is nearly dry, scrunch up with hands to increase curl.

5. Tong individual curls to achieve more definition.

6. Work all over head in same way.

7. Take a triangular section at front.

8. Twist, but not too tightly, to form a coil.

9. Allow coil to loop into a loose curl.

10. Grip in place.

11. Repeat all over head, making coils and gripping into place.

12. Mist finished style with hairspray.

OPPOSITE Dress: Renato Nucci at Moda Rosa, Alresford, Hants
Hair accessory: Irresistible Headdresses

PERSEPHONE

1. Before.

2. Take large sections and smooth using a jumbo tong to add slight movement.

3. Part hair in centre and smooth behind ears.

4. From centre back take first section and twist, not too tightly.

5. Loop upwards to crown and grip in place, leaving end out.

6. Shows first loop gripped in place.

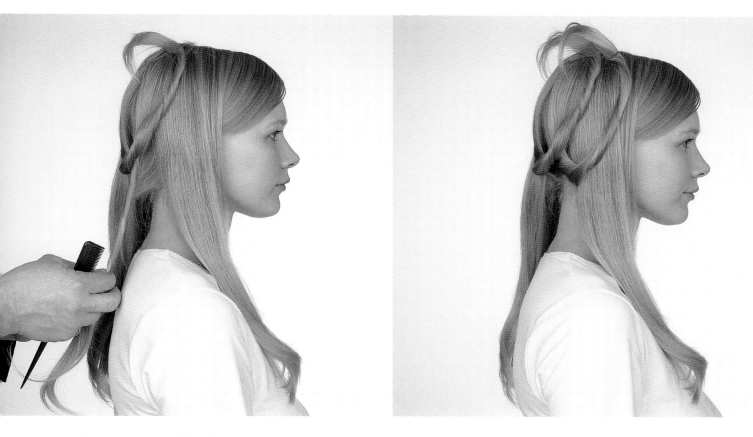

7. Take next section, parallel to first, and twist in same way.

8. Loop upwards to crown and grip in place.

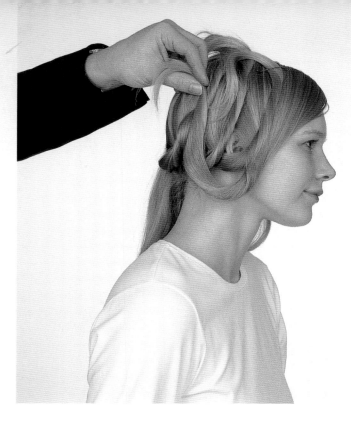

9. Take next section and work in same way.

10. Take front second, work in same way but loop backwards round ear.

11. Curl and pin ends of each loop.

12. Shows one side completed, work other side in same way but bring all coils round to first side.

OPPOSITE Dress and wrap: Amanda Wakeley at Moda Rosa, Alresford, Hants
Hair accessory: Irresistible Headdresses

ANGELINA

1. Before.

2. Smooth hair, section by section, using straightening irons.

3. Hair completely straightened.

4. Diagonally part hair from temple to nape, then use a grooming brush to smooth hair back.

5. Shows other side.

6. Clasp hair in ponytail at centre back.

7. Secure hair in covered band.

8. Take a small section of hair, wrap round band and secure with a grip.

9. Twist ponytail in a clockwise direction, using both hands, until it coils round.

10. Secure with grips.

11. Backcomb fringe gently.

12. Loop fringe round finger into a barrel curl and secure.

OPPOSITE Dress: Clements Ribeiro at Moda Rosa, Alresford, Hants

LILY

1. Before.

2. Use a grooming brush to smooth hair into a ponytail at side of head.

3. Secure using a covered band.

4. Take one section from ponytail and tong.

5. Repeat until all ponytail hair is tonged.

6. Thread ponytail through centre of a bun ring

7. Secure bun ring using grips

8. Take a section of ponytail hair.

9. Loop into curl allowing end to fall free.

10. Grip into place.

11. Shape ends of curl onto padding and pin in place.

12. Continue making curls in same way, pinning into place as you work.

OPPOSITE Dress: Betzer Johnson at Moda Rosa, Alresford, Hants
Hair accessory: Irresistible Headdresses

MARIELLA

1. Before.

2. Brush hair to crown and use a covered band to secure in a high ponytail.

3. Tong ponytail hair a section at a time.

4. Thread ponytail through bun ring and secure. Thread on a second bun ring

5. Push this second bun ring forward and secure at base.

6. Take a 5cm section from ponytail, loop into a curl.

7. Twist and grip as shown.

8. Curl ends into another curl and grip.

9. Shows first completed curl.

10. Continue making first round of curls in same way, then start second layer.

11. Pin second layer of curls on top of first layer of curls.

12. Mist with hairspray.

OPPOSITE Dress: Ralph Lauren at Moda Rosa, Alresford, Hants
Hair accessory: Irresistible Headdresses

SERENITY

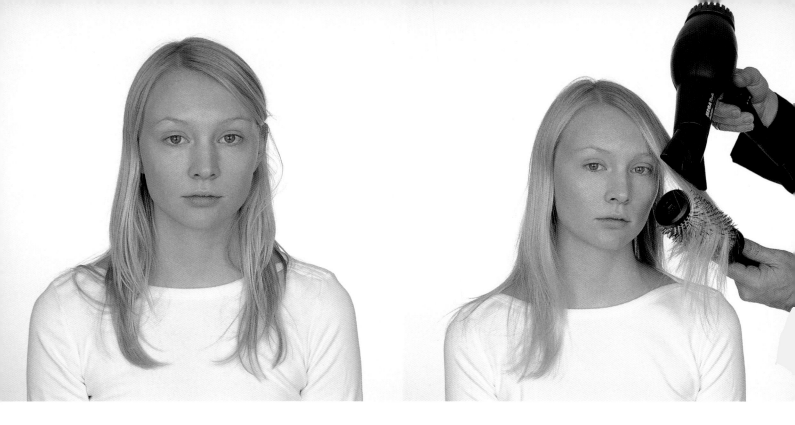

1. Before.

2. Smooth hair using concentrator nozzle on hairdryer and a hot curl brush.

3. Use straightening irons to flatten hair a section at a time.

4. Apply serum through hair to smooth cuticle and add shine.

5. Section off front hair then take section from behind ear.

6. Loop this section of hair.

7. Form into a knot.

8. Pull knot upwards.

9. Secure with a grip, leaving ends loose.

10. Shows first completed knot. Work round occipital bone in same manner.

11. Work other curls in same manner.

12. Finish by taking front reserved section of hair and tying to underneath section in a double knot.

OPPOSITE Dress: Edina Ronay at Moda Rosa, Alresford, Hants

Hairdressing And Beauty Industry Authority series – related titles

HAIRDRESSING

Art of Hair Colouring by David Adams and Jacki Wadeson
Bridal Hair by Pat Dixon and Jacki Wadeson
Essensuals, Next Generation Toni & Guy Step by Step
Mahogany Hairdressing: Advanced Looks by Richard Thompson and Martin Gannon
Mahogany Hairdressing: Steps to Cutting, Colouring and Finishing Hair by Martin Gannon and
   Richard Thompson
Patrick Cameron: Dressing Long Hair by Patrick Cameron and Jacki Wadeson
Patrick Cameron: Dressing Long Hair Book 2 by Patrick Cameron
Professional Men's Hairdressing by Guy Kremer and Jacki Wadeson
The Total Look: The Style Guide for Hair and Make-Up Professionals by Ian Mistlin
Trevor Sorbie: Visions in Hair by Kris Sorbie and Jacki Wadeson

African-Caribbean Hairdressing, 2e by Sandra Gittens
Hairdressing – The Foundations: The Official Guide to Level 2 by Leo Palladino
Men's Hairdressing: Traditional and Modern Barbering by Maurice Lister
Professional Hairdressing: The Official Guide to Level 3 by Martin Green, Leo Palladino
   and Theresa Bullock
Salon Management by Martin Green
Start Hairdressing: The Official Guide to Level 1 by Martin Green and Leo Palladino
The World of Hair: A Scientific Companion by Dr John Gray

BEAUTY THERAPY

An Holistic Guide to Anatomy & Physiology by Tina Parsons
An Holistic Guide to Reflexology by Tina Parsons
Aromatherapy for the Beauty Therapist by Valerie Ann Worwood
Beauty Therapy – The Foundations: The Official Guide to Level 2 by Lorraine Nordmann
Indian Head Massage by Muriel Burnham-Airey and Adele O'Keefe
Nail Artistry by Jacqui Jefford, Sue Marsh and Ann Swain
Nutrition by Suzanne Le Quesne
Professional Beauty Therapy: The Official Guide to Level 3 by Lorraine Nordmann, Lorraine
   Appleyard and Pamela Linforth
Safety in the Salon by Elaine Almond
The Complete Nail Technician by Marian Newman
The Encyclopedia of Nails by Jacqui Jefford and Anne Swain
The Official Guide to Body Massage by Adele O'Keefe
The World of Skin Care: A Scientific Companion by Dr John Gray

Guildford College
Learning Resource Centre

Please return on or before the last date shown.
No further issues or renewals if any items are overdue.
"7 Day" loans are **NOT** renewable.

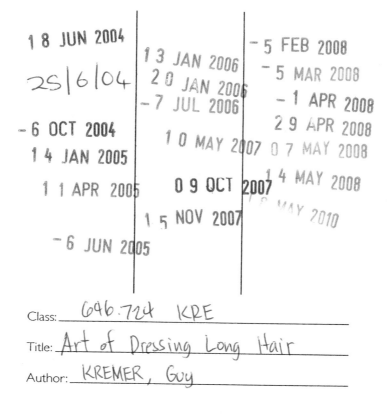

1 8 JUN 2004

25/6/04

1 3 JAN 2006
2 0 JAN 2006
- 7 JUL 2006

- 5 FEB 2008
- 5 MAR 2008
- 1 APR 2008

- 6 OCT 2004
1 4 JAN 2005

1 0 MAY 2007

2 9 APR 2008
0 7 MAY 2008

1 1 APR 2005

0 9 OCT 2007

1 4 MAY 2008

1 5 NOV 2007

8 MAY 2010

- 6 JUN 2005

Class: 646.724 KRE

Title: Art of Dressing Long Hair

Author: KREMER, Guy

**7 DAY
BOOK**